LOST IN THE FOREST

. If you are on a hill, always go downhill. At best you will come across water (rivulet, stream, river). If you follow this, you will inevitably come across inhabited areas at some point.

If you are lost in the lowlands, go straight ahead until you are out of the forest, or until you reach a path.

Be oriented to the sun, to the mossy side of the trees (northwest) and to the thicker annual rings of the trees (south).

Ideally, you have a pocket compass with you. Of course, rarely anyone carries it with them. If you are in nature a lot, then this belongs to the basic equipment.

It is advantageous if you can determine the cardinal points. Often forests are real primeval forests and "going straight" is simply impossible. If you have to change direction all the time, even a small forest can be your undoing.

INJURIES IN THE FOREST

The death cap mushroom grows in mixed and deciduous forests and is deadly. After about 20 hours, cramping abdominal pain, nausea and vomiting diarrhea plague you. However, this then seems to get better, but then the symptoms return more severely, with kidney and liver damage. This leads to death within 3-8 days if left untreated. However, if the poisoning is detected early enough, it can be treated with a substance derived from milk thistle. Giant hogweed, also called Hercules perennial, can grow up to 3.5 meters high. In contact with the skin and subsequent exposure to the sun, very painful sores appear, which are like severe burns.

ANIMAL ATTACK IN THE FOREST

Most forest animals are shy and will keep away from us humans as much as possible. However, there are exceptions that can become very unpleasant for hikers, for example game that defends their young or the territory, wild boars, rabid foxes, badgers, wolves and bears.

Surprising swarms of wasps or hornets can be a race for hikers. The only thing that helps is to run, or to take refuge in the water (stream, river, pond) and submerge yourself if there is water nearby. Many other insects such as mosquitoes, horseflies and also spiders can give us nasty bites or stings. It is therefore important not to leave sweet drinks or food lying around openly, otherwise camping in the forest can become dangerous. It is also advisable to always have insect repellent and ointment or gel for insect bites in your luggage for initial treatment.

If a storm comes up while you're out in the forest, it's important to get out of the forest as quickly as possible, find shelter in a cave or a hut, or at least find a clearing where you'll be safe from breaking branches and falling and uprooted trees.

During thunderstorms, you are in mortal danger in the forest. Therefore, the first thing to do is to check the weather forecast to see if there is a risk of thunderstorms. If a thunderstorm should still surprise you, the lightning always strikes the highest elevation. Therefore, you should never stand under a single tree or seek shelter at the edge of a forest.

If you have no possibility to get out of the forest, then you might be safest in the middle of the forest.

Caution! If lightning strikes a tree near you, the electromagnetic discharge that accompanies it can also expand in the ground around the tree. In any case, this wave can cause life-threatening damage to the cardiovascular system in humans

The risk of forest fires has increased in recent years due to the increasingly dry and hot weather. A carelessly discarded cigarette, broken glass, or a campfire are often enough to start a forest fire. It is our sole responsibility to treat nature with care and not to throw away any garbage.

HOW LONG CAN YOU SURVIVE WITHOUT WATER?

How long you can survive without water depends on several factors: age, health status, temperature, humidity and physical activity. This means a young, healthy person will survive without hydration for about 3-4 days before the body's toxins cause organ failure, a stroke, or heart failure.

Can you die of thirst in the snow? Yes really, you can! Because if you can't melt the snow, you can never get enough water just by "eating snow".

You would have to eat at least 10 kilograms of snow to get 1 liter of water from it. Even if you can melt the snow with a stove or something similar, this could still lead to dehydration over time, because due to the lack of mineral salts in the snow, the body soon reacts to it with vomiting, headaches, heart palpitations and nausea, sometimes even coma and death. However, if you have enough food reserves with you, then you don't have to worry about that.

SURVIVING A BEAR ATTACK

Normally, the bear hibernates. As temperatures continue to rise, bears are awakening from hibernation much earlier. A devastating cycle. Due to the early awakening, the animals find nothing to eat and become more and more aggressive. The most dangerous bears are in spring because they are hungry.

What to do when you see a bear
in the wild (or it sees you)?

Do not panic! The bear will probably
get out of your way before you notice it.

If you are in a bear area, a bear bell is standard equipment. The bell rings when you move and will warn the bear. Alternatively, you can also speak calmly, whistle or sing to draw the bear's attention to you.

If the bear comes towards you, walk slowly backwards and keep talking. The most important thing, however, is the bear spray, which you should always have at hand on a carabiner in the belt loop, ready for immediate use.

Do not make threatening gestures and do not
try to scare the bear away. This only makes
the animals aggressive, because it is perceived
as a threat. If you discover fresh bear tracks
such as footprints or droppings, then
immediately retreat from the area calmly.
You can talk or ring your bear bell.

If the bear cannot be deterred, for example because it is curious, or a problem bear, then it is always a good idea to be equipped with a bear spray.

A bear is a fast runner! In case you're wondering if you can outrun a bear while running: No, you can't! Running away is therefore a bad idea. The bear is faster in any case.

A bear is a good climber (black bear). And if he doesn't climb, he's good at knocking down trees (grizzly)! That's why you shouldn't try to climb the next tree if possible.

Mother bears see every intruder as a threat! If the bear goes on the attack even though you're playing dead, it's probably because it sees you as food. The rule here is: defend with all means! Aim for the bear's nose and eyes, because they are the most sensitive.

Bears have a keen sense of smell and a soft spot for our food. Therefore, never leave food scraps lying around. Never hang garbage on a tree. If you are camping, burn or bury your food after the meal. If you are in a bear area, it is mandatory to carry an airtight and break open proof container. This should be stored at least 50 meters or more from the campsite, about 4 meters above the ground on a tree. This is the place to cook and eat. You should never eat where you sleep!

Black bears and grizzly bears are very different in their behavior. Therefore, you should be able to identify the bear you are facing.

Black bears are smaller than grizzlies and good climbers. If a black bear attacks, it will jump on you and try to bite into your head or shoulder and rip you open with its claws. Use your trekking poles and bear spray. If you don't have anything handy, try to defend yourself with rocks and sticks, a knife or other weapons. Black bears are also excellent climbers, so do not take refuge in a tree.

Grizzly bears are bigger and heavier. If you fight back, it will make them even angrier. The grizzly will most likely run towards you at high speed and then build up in front of you. Then it will strike with its paw. If you have a weapon, the best chance is to use it now, before it hits you with its paw. If you don't have a weapon, the best chance to survive is to play dead. To do this, lie flat on your stomach, face down, put your hands on the back of your neck (protection) and stop moving and try not to scream. People who have survived a grizzly attack report that the grizzly did not leave them until they stopped screaming and played dead.

TIPS IN A WILD BOAR ENCOUNTER

From November the mating season begins. Male boars can sometimes react more aggressively during this time. From March to May, the sows usually give birth to their young and react sensitively to troublemakers during this time. If you see wild boar piglets (shoats), then avoid any contact and turn back immediately! The mother animal is in the immediate vicinity!

Public areas such as playgrounds and parks often harbor irresistible food resources for wild boars. Full trash cans and carelessly discarded food scraps are a veritable land of milk and honey for them. Usually, wild boars flee before we get to see them. Since urban wild boars are less afraid of humans, the approach distance can be reduced to 10 to 5 meters. This also reduces the attack distance! Children often underestimate this danger and keep too little distance.

Wild boars can inflict life-threatening injuries with their tusks. They also have razor-sharp teeth and can really bite! If you encounter a wild boar with its tail up, fixating on you, snorting loudly through its nose, and perhaps chattering its teeth and wagging its head, this is a sign that it is about to attack.

What to do in case of wild boar attack? Pull back slowly and avoid hectic movements. Do not deny the animal its way out and allow it to retreat. If the wild boar runs at you confusedly, then it can be that it feels the danger, but cannot see you because of its bad view. Here you can clap your hands or shout loudly. If possible, climb a tree or a high stand or take refuge in the heights. Running away is not an option: Wild boars can reach speeds of up to 50 km/h. The animal will try to attack your legs or run between your legs.

THE RIGHT BEHAVIOR IN A WOLF ENCOUNTER

If you are in a wolf area, you should be aware that wolves do not only hide in the deep forest. On the contrary, they prefer forest roads to save energy. Crossing deep forests, wet or swampy areas or areas with deep foliage or high grass are energy robbers. Now, if you spot a wolf and he hasn't seen or heard you, you should slowly and quietly back up and move out of his territory. Keep an eye on him as best you can and watch to see if he follows you.

Should you surprise a cub or a very curious wolf, he may come toward you. Wolves that have been fed are more likely to follow you curiously. Now, first and foremost, you should remain calm and stop. If you are jogging or biking, stop and get off your bike, because wolves are hunters and fast movements activate their hunting instinct. Attention: A fast escape is not an option. You will never be faster than the wolf and thus only stimulate its hunting instinct!

This is the best opportunity to put your self-confidence to the test. Be confident. Stand up straight, shoulders back, head up, stomach in. Imagine you are called to your boss and don't want to show him that you are shaking inside!

Show your fortitude! Stand with your legs wide apart. Don't stand there as if the slightest breeze could blow you.

Make noise by singing loudly! If you meet a wolf who has not yet noticed you you can draw attention to yourself in this way - more or less elegantly.

Clap your hands. Supportively, you can also loudly shout "Get lost! Je Taime!, or shout "Help, Mommy!". Whatever comes to your mind in this situation. The wolf will not understand your words, but your intention.

Animal repellent sprays are not only effective against bear attacks. If the wolf is not intimidated after all your previous measures, but continues to pester you, then you can use the animal repellent spray. The wolf will be violently distracted by the spray and will feel a burning sensation. Now slowly move away, because you've bought yourself enough time to escape. The animal repellent spray will of course make the wolf very uncomfortable, but will not cause it any permanent damage.

In the event of a wolf encounter with a hiking group, everyone present should stay together in any case. Children and dogs should be taken into the middle or on the arm. If the wolf is hungry or cannot be intimidated, it will focus first and foremost on the smallest members of the group. Under no circumstances should the group break apart, or some group members move in another direction, or the group try to encircle the wolf, because this could make the wolf feel insecure or constricted.

A wolf cannot be dangerous to a horse? Wrong! The correct behavior in case of wolf contact with horse is to stop and dismount. Not because the wolf might pounce on the horse, but so you don't fall off the horse if it gets nervous or spooked. Horses in wolf areas should be desensitized from an early age so that a wolf encounter does not end in trauma for both horse and rider.

Wolves are true survivors and tough when it comes to injuries. Almost like cats, they seem to have nine lives. So if you find an injured animal or hit a wolf with your car, leave it alone and call in the official veterinarian or the nature conservation authority. They will then take care of the injured animal. Also, according to experts, an injured or sick wolf is not dangerous. Normally, his pack will take care of him.

Should you stumble upon a wolf den during one of your adventure tours in the deep forest, then immediately retreat. Calmly and slowly. This is not at all about the wolf attacking you, but that he might leave his offspring behind out of fear. Maybe you will meet a wolf howling or making barking sounds. This is his way of telling you that you are not welcome. The wolf will follow you for a while or will not let you out of its sight. Watch the wolf out of the corner of your eye as you move away from the cave.

The best way to avoid wolf encounters on your
camping trip is to carefully dispose of all leftovers
after your meal, far away from your campsite.
Leaving your leftovers in plain sight, or hanging your
garbage bag on the nearest tree, is tantamount to
inviting wolves, as well as other wildlife, in. Wolves
have a highly developed sense of smell and travel
great distances in search of food. So when you
unwrap your fried chicken or burger, chances are a
wolf can smell them over a mile away.

Control your throwing arm. Do not throw objects around, because that could make the wolf curious.

Running away is a very bad idea, because wolves have hunting instincts, which you activate with your escape. Even if you are a fast runner: The healthy wolf is always faster!

Love does not go through the stomach! In your panic, do not under any circumstances try to feed the wolf. It is also not appropriate to leave the animal your leftover hamburger.

Don't play dead! This might work for bear attacks, but wolves are different. They go by the motto "kill first", which means that they pursue their prey with only one goal in mind, and that is to prey.

Don't look me in the eye, baby! Don't stare and avoid looking directly into the eyes of your animal counterpart. Wolves see this as a challenge.

When you move away from the wolf, it is best to move slowly backwards, but without looking directly at the wolf. If you turn your back to the wolf, it may be that he is encouraged to follow you.

Wolves are pack animals. So unless you're encountering a lone wolf, it's very likely that the wolf you're seeing is not alone, and more eyes are on you than you suspect. That's why it's even more important to remember the following: No matter what - running away is not an option! Wolves hunt in packs and kill their prey as they run. If you run away, the pack will chase you.